Do Not Forget What Your Eyes Have Seen

— Deut. 4 —

Do Not Forget What Your Eyes Have Seen

— Deut. 4 —

Shirley Miller, RSCJ

Society of the Sacred Heart

Saint Louis, Missouri

Do Not Forget What Your Eyes Have Seen
Shirley Miller, RSCJ

Copyright ©2020 Society of the Sacred Heart. All rights reserved. No part of this book may be used or reproduced by any means, graphic, electronic, or mechanical, including photocopying, recording, taping or by any information storage retrieval system without the written permission of the editor except in the case of brief quotations embodied in articles and reviews.

Photos by Shirley Miller, RSCJ

Printed in the United States of America
ISBN-13: 978-0-9971329-9-1

Published by:

Society of the Sacred Heart™
United States – Canada

4120 Forest Park Avenue
St. Louis Missouri 63108-2809
314-652-1500
RSCJ.org

*To the Society of the Sacred Heart
and the family of the Sacred Heart,
and all who have inspired me.*

*To my sisters Mary Dell Barkouras and
Carolyn Smith who continually astonish me
with their love and faith and in gratitude for their
sisterhood, friendship and support.*

Contents

Walk gently and love tenderly.

All of life is a gift, precious, fragile, and vulnerable.

Introduction

WHEN I WAS A CHILD, I kept a diary and wrote all of my most personal thoughts each day, and I locked it with a key each night so my siblings would not be able to read it. As a child, I borrowed (or sometimes I took it when Dad was at work!) my Dad's camera, and I wandered a few blocks away up in the hills to see through the eye of the camera. All of my life words and images have led to deeper places where God seemed to be saying, "Stop, look, listen…"

Photography is a way of praying, "of witnessing the wonder" (Abraham Heschel). The camera provides an opening into the eternal for me, the lifting of the veil, the long view, the up close, the panorama. It is a healing prayer for me. At times of discouragement, weariness or confusion, when I walk on the beach or wander in a garden or on a mountainside or stop by the side of the road to watch the wind in the Kansas wheat fields or sunlight breaking through the window of an abandoned farm house, I experience deep peace.

The sacredness of creation overflows everywhere: the barren tree against the winter sky, the morning dew on a dandelion, the red cardinal resting on a moss-covered branch, the eagle soaring high above the trees, the morning star in the dark sky, the great blue heron standing erect at the sea's edge. The camera helps me understand the connectedness of all creation and my part in it. Each action of mine somehow mysteriously affects the entire universe. Photography is a way for me to experience

God's immaculate conception of the world – all is holy, all is sacred. My only response can be "gratefulness for witnessing the wonder" (Abraham Heschel).

These photos and reflections are part my journey from childhood to old age, of fifty-five years as a Religious of the Sacred Heart, forty of those years as a teacher and administrator in three Sacred Heart Schools – Woodlands Academy in Lake Forest, Illinois, Duchesne Academy in Omaha, and the Academy of the Sacred Heart, the Rosary in New Orleans – and in the past fifteen years in the mission advancement office for the Society of the Sacred Heart in St. Louis. I am deeply grateful for the people I have met along the road, for the Society of the Sacred Heart, for the places I have seen, for the relationships that have transformed my life, for my family who has loved and encouraged me and for our faithful God who has led me through the peaks and valleys, storms and calm, encouraging me always, to "Not forget what my eyes have seen…"

—*Shirley Miller, RSCJ*

Section 1

Gifts from the Sea

Gift from the Sea

A STROLL ON THE BEACH in late November. I walked by two little children collecting shells. They looked at me, smiled and asked me if I was finding any shells. I said I was just out walking toward the sunset, and I asked them what shells they had found. "Look at this one," and I say, "That's a moon shell." He shows me another one, and I say, "That one is a channeled whelk." And another one, I say, "That's an oyster shell." The oldest child says, "You sure do know a lot about shells." And I say, "I learned a lot about them from reading a book, *Gift from the Sea*." "Oh, yeah, our mom brings it to the beach every year but she never reads it." "When you go back to your condo, tell your mom it is really worth reading."

A stroll on the beach next evening. I feel a presence behind me. I turn to a woman who says, "Thanks a lot." I realize it is the boys' mother. "Did you bring *Gift from the Sea* with you this time?" "Yes, I always bring it." "Well, on this dark and gloomy day, why don't you begin it this evening?" She smiles and goes inside.

A stroll on the beach next evening. I feel the presence. It is the children's mother. "Thanks a lot," she says, and this time she really means it. "I wish I had read it a few years ago instead of reading all those novels. It might have helped me save my marriage. But it might not be too late to save myself." "What's wrong with novels?" I inquire. "They are too much like my real life." We hug; I continue my walk; she goes back to her condo.

Each morning for the next week I saw her walking the beach, carrying *Gift from the Sea* and I prayed that it was not too late for her to save herself.

An Easter Apparition

SEVERAL YEARS AGO, some friends gave me a week at Seaside Village in Florida for Holy Week and Easter. I was driving back to New Orleans early afternoon on Easter. As I drove by Graton Beach, with the white sand and sea oats and the emerald sea, I knew I had to stop and spend a few quiet hours in this exquisite place. A few families were on the beach. I carried my chair down close to the water, far enough away from the families so I could enjoy the solitude...until seven-year-old Lily walked over and sat on the sand beside me, and hugged my legs. I smiled and said, "I am Shirley. Who are you?" She grinned but said nothing. She just sat in the sand and hugged my legs and rested her head on my knees.

After a while Lily's mother walked over to me and told me that Lily has autism, that she has never spoken a word. But she has a mission in life: she cannot stand to see anyone alone. She wants to keep them company. A child who cannot use words or express what she needs is concerned about another's aloneness. I wept quietly as she rested her head on my knees. Lily's mother went back to her place on the beach. A little while later, Lily's parents came to pick her up to play with her in the waves. When I folded up my chair to return to the road, Lily looked back from the water and blew me a kiss, and I returned it.

Lily! An Easter apparition – not at the Sea of Galilee but at Graton Beach – a memory that will stay in my heart forever. May each of us, like Lily, discover our mission in life. Perhaps it is simply being with others when they feel alone.

Johnny Cash

WALKING ON THE BEACH IN Gulf Shores, Alabama, caught up in the glory and beauty of the sunset, I was shell collecting, fragments of all colors and sizes. A Johnny Cash looking man, dressed all in black, approached me and asked if I was finding anything beautiful. I showed him my bag filled with exquisite fragments. His hands were filled with perfect shells, and he said, "Take whatever you would like to have. They are all gifts from God meant to be given away." I looked into his deeply lined face as he held out his hands to me. I carefully selected a few precious treasures. I thanked him and offered him my fragments. He took several, and we said good night. As walked away I sang softly Johnny Cash's famous song, "Man in Black."

I walked the beach every night, but I never saw him again. His one-time appearance was a "gift from the sea." I continue to collect shells of all shapes, sizes and colors, giving thanks to God for the perfect ones, the fragments, the old ones tossed and turned by the waves. My collection will always hold the perfect ones from the Man in Black. He will always remind me of the words he spoke to me and which God continues to speak to me, "They are all gifts from God, meant to be given away."

Let us all generously share the gifts we have been given, even with strangers we meet along the way.

Dawn and the Sacred Heart of Jesus

ONE PRE-DAWN MORNING during my retreat in Gulf Shores, Alabama, I was given a gift: as the black sky turned into dawn, the morning light pierced through the darkness and poured light out upon the entire sea. It was more than dawn beginning another day. It was the love of the pierced Heart of Christ poured out on the entire world. St. Madeleine Sophie, the foundress of the Society of the Sacred Heart, wrote long ago, "Our little Society was born when Jesus's heart was pierced on the cross, and blood and water flowed out."

Signs, symbols, and sacramentals have the power to draw us into the deepest realities of our faith whether they be a sign in the sky, a pierced heart on RSCJ profession crosses, on Children of Mary medals or class rings, sweatshirts or water glasses. They are all reminders of the love of the Heart of Christ poured out on each of us and on our world and of our call to share that love with all whom we encounter.

Cor Unum et Anima Una, one heart and one soul in the Heart of Jesus, is the motto of the Society of the Sacred Heart.

How fortunate we are to have such symbols that we can touch and hold and grasp onto in times of great need and in moments of deep thanksgiving. How blessed we are to witness God's beauty in the sky, over the sea and in one another's hearts.

Sunglasses on the Beach

I WAS WALKING THE BEACH after a tropical storm, and I came across a pair of women's sunglasses covered with barnacles, obviously in the sea for a long time, washed up on the shore. I picked them up and reflected on the person who had lost them. Was she swept away in another storm? What had her eyes seen during her lifetime? Is she walking the beach looking for her lost glasses?

Her glasses challenged me to look more deeply, to give thanks for the person whose glasses I had found. Each gift from the sea is precious, a revelation, and an inspiration.

Wherever you are, I pray for you often. Thank you for your gift.

"Do not forget the things your eyes have seen nor let them slip from your heart all the days of your life" Deut. 4:9.

Stop, look, listen. You never know what gift from the sea is waiting for you.

Wow Is Worth Waiting For

RECENTLY I WAS WALKING the beach at sunset. A father and son were gazing up at the setting sun. The father walked into the waves, and his young son stood on the shore, impatient. As I walked by, the father came out of the waves and said to me, "I feel silly, a middle-aged man searching for sand dollars." I smiled and said, "I am an older woman doing the same thing." We laughed and he returned to the waves.

I stood in the surf, my net digging deeply in search of shells. His son called out to him, "Come on, Dad, let's go to McDonald's. We can buy sand dollars and sunset post cards on the way home." With these words, the father emerged from the waves, put his arm around him and said, "Son, there are some things that money can't buy. You have to search for the things that have the most meaning." The son shrugged his arm off his shoulder. A few minutes later the father leapt out of the water with a large sand dollar in his hand. "Here son, take this to your mother and wish her a happy birthday." "Wow!" said the son, and off he ran, clutching the treasure in his hand. The father called after him, "Son, don't forget to watch the sunset."

Let us pray for one another as we continue to search together for those things that money cannot buy, as we continue to be filled with awe as we look at the setting sun, as we embrace one another with love. Let us be like the father on the beach, searching deeply when it might be easier to stand on the shore and risk looking silly.

WOW is worth waiting for!

The Great Blue Heron

I GREW UP IN NEBRASKA AND IOWA, the land of Canada geese stopping to feast in the fields before flying South for the winter. Beautiful as they were, flying in formation through the sunrise, honking in unison, when I flew South to live for many years, I became completely enchanted by the great blue heron. The silent and elegant bird, standing at sea's edge for long periods of time, looking for breakfast. Wherever there was a fisherman, there was the blue heron. I was awed by its majesty, its wingspan, its grace, its mystery. The heron became a sign of the presence of God for me—at dawn in the scarlet sky, at dusk in the golden sunset—calling me to notice, to be present, to pray.

Each morning at the beach, I arise before dawn to enter into the unfolding of a new day. I go out on the balcony, and there he is on the shore below, standing erect, also welcoming a new day. Often he flies up past my balcony and flies farther down the beach and inviting me to follow. At sunset we walk together, he a few steps in front of me or sometimes right beside me.

The last time I saw him on the shore, he and a fisherman were standing together. I had a new insight. Perhaps I am now the heron, and Jesus is the fisherman, inviting me to stay close, trusting that I will receive whatever grace I need for the day. I live in St. Louis now, away from the sea. Sometimes when I go to Forest Park and sit by the little ponds, he appears, reminding me that I am not forgotten, and graces for the day continue to be abundant.

What is your symbol for God?

The Red Bucket

SEVERAL YEARS AGO I had finished a major project, and I had a three week break. I was tired and felt weary. I drove to the Gulf Shore. As I walked the beach at sunset my first night there, I saw a child's red bucket lying on its side in the sand. The little bucket gave me words for what I was feeling. I continued my walk into the sunset, asking God to lift me out of the sand, to help me stand up and continue my journey.

When I walked back to the condo, I went to the red bucket to say thank you for the grace it was to me. It was filled with golden light from the setting sun. A transformation. I, too, felt transformed. If God can fill a little red bucket with golden light, certainly God will do the same for me.

When I returned to my room, I felt replenished, feeling deeply grateful for those moments and for the little child who left the bucket on the beach. The next morning when I walked at sunrise, the red bucket was gone, perhaps washed out to the sea at high tide or down to another spot on the beach to find another person who needed a transformation.

"Anything can speak to us of God if we are attentive enough." [author unknown]

A friend gave me a little red bucket when I returned home. It reminds me as I come in and out of my room many times a day to be attentive and to be grateful.

Christmas, Incarnation and the Perfect Shell

CHRISTMAS, INCARNATION. God chose to dwell among us, human and vulnerable as we are, exposed to all of life's agonies and ecstacies.

I was at Ship Island for the day. As I walked along the beach, I saw a perfect shell. I picked it up, admired it and knew I had to take this one home with me. I returned to the large log, washed up from the sea, where I had left my Bible and journal, and placed it on the log and continued my walk. When I returned the shell had fallen into the sand. I picked it up and put it back on the log. It fell off again. It was only then that I realized the shell was inhabited by a hermit crab that was trying to get back to the sea.

I realized how selfish I was — wanting the shell for myself when the crab needed the shell for protection to return to the sea. I took it close to the water, and said, "Goodbye beautiful shell, good luck, little crab, with your journey back to the sea." The crab in its borrowed shell crawled back toward me, and right there in front of me, it crawled out of the shell, and exposed to the heat and hot sand, vulnerable to attacks by sea gulls, and began its slow journey back to the sea.

The moment of watching that little crab emptying itself, giving its borrowed home up to me, will be with me forever. I had a new understanding of the Incarnation, the Word Made Flesh, God choosing to strip God-ness and become human like us.

Jesus said, "What I have done for you, so you must do for one another." What am I willing to leave behind?

Please, Ma'am, Don't Walk on the Shells

DEVOTION TO THE SACRED HEART OF JESUS is incarnational, relational and transformational. We are called to invite God's love to transform our own hearts into hearts of love and to allow that love to flow freely from our hearts out to others. "Our call is to contemplate the Heart of Christ in the pierced heart of humanity." (Society of the Sacred Heart, Chapter 1970)

The pierced Heart of Jesus in humanity is especially evident today. The need for love and respect is all around us – in our homes, communities, offices, schools, streets and screens. Our great responsibility is to take care of the heart, God's Heart in the world, our own hearts, the hearts of one another, and the hearts of those who have lost hope.

Several years ago I was walking the beach in Gulf Shores, Alabama. A little boy came from behind me, tugged at my jacket and said, "Please, Ma'am, don't walk on the shells. You will hurt them." My eyes filled with tears. I took his hand and said, "Thank you." He led me back to the sand, away from the beach. He said, "You can walk here because the sand cushions the shells."

The child taught me about the love of the Heart of Christ that morning: to walk gently and to love tenderly. All of life is a gift, precious, fragile, vulnerable. Each person created in God's image deserves our compassion and respect. Take care of the heart.

Section 2

Other Reflections

Bella

SEVERAL YEARS AGO, a four-year-old Pre-Kindergarten child asked me for an appointment. She wanted to become an RSCJ and wanted to know how to go about it. She came to my office for a lunch meeting. My office was BIG, and she walked around touching everything. I had an eighteenth century Bible on my coffee table. She opened it and paged through it and came to a print of the crucifixion. She said, "What is that?" I told her that Jesus was being crucified. Bella said, "That must have hurt him a lot. Sister Miller, have you ever been crucified?" A poignant question during a challenging time in my life. How do you explain to a four year old? "No, Bella, not like Jesus, but all of us have suffering in our life, and Jesus helps us get through it."

I asked her why she wanted to become a nun. She said she wanted to pray all the time. I told her that nuns also have to work a lot. And she quipped back, "Sister Miller, don't you know after all this time of being a nun that you can pray and work at the same time?" Out of the mouths of babes...

Bella is a grown woman now. She is a critical care nurse in New Orleans, and I have no doubt that she continues to work and pray at the same time.

Molly's Magic

MANY YEARS AGO, when I was headmistress at the Academy of the Sacred Heart, the Rosary, New Orleans, I was having a particularly challenging day. Preschool children always lifted me up, so I walked over to the Preschool play yard, and a child named Molly was holding a pie tin of sand, dirt and leaves. I asked her what she was doing. She said she was making magic. "You want some magic, Sister Miller?" "Yes, Molly, I need some magic." She said, "Come sit by me in the sandbox and close your eyes and make a wish." I did as Molly instructed me to do! She waited a few moments and then said, "Have you made your wish?" I made a huge wish that I thought might even be beyond God's help! "Are you ready for the magic?" asked Molly. "Yes, I am ready." Molly poured her tin of magic over my head, covering me and my black suit with sand, dirt and leaves.

I felt a deep grace flow through my entire being. Molly said, "Open your eyes, Sister Miller. Did you get your wish?" "Oh, yes, Molly. More than I can possibly tell you." Molly invited me back for more magic whenever I need it!

I shook the sand out of my hair, brushed it off my suit, hugged her and thanked her and went to a meeting that I was dreading… but the dread was gone. I was covered with Molly's magic. Whenever I need to be covered with magic, I think of Molly, and the magic returns.

Green Soap

RECENTLY I WAS in an airport rest room. A mother and small child walked in. And the child said, enthusiastically, "Look, Mom. They have green soap. I love green soap." Her mother lifted her up to the sink, and the child lavishly covered her hands and arms with green soap. I said that I like green soap, too. We smiled at each other. They left and I started to leave when an older woman walked in to wash her hands and said, "I hate green soap!" and she left without washing her hands.

Our lives would be so much more beautiful if we could embrace the diversity of our world. The beach would be so much less enchanting if it was covered only with sand dollars; the sky so much less glorious if there were no clouds; the ocean less dramatic if it was always low tide. How incomplete our churches and streets and neighborhoods would be if there were only white people. How good of God to create such diversity in all of creation. I love pansies but without the rose, the petunia, the hibiscus, the gardenia our gardens would be so much less beautiful and fragrant. Only when we embrace the differences among us and within us, only when we embrace the wholeness of God's creation will RESURRECTION truly happen. I saw a poster once that said, "It is by your differences that you enrich me."

Maybe when we really look at and listen to one another, we will learn to love green soap or at least be respectful toward those who do.

Carmel Cross

A FEW YEARS AGO, I was on a fund raising adventure in California. I drove along the coast on my way to Carmel, and I was astonished at what I was seeing and experiencing. It was a perfect California day, warm, blue sky and white clouds, no wind – just spectacular beauty as far as my eye could see. I pulled off the road several times, got out of the car, and sat on the massive rocks, giving thanks for God's magnificent creation.

I made my third stop by several stark and petrified trees. One tree in particular drew me, suggesting that I spend the rest of my time just where I was.

This is the image that I saw: for me it was the crucified Christ, with the light of resurrection pouring out from his face.

St. Paul writes in 2 Corinthians: "For God who said, 'Let light shine out of darkness, made his light shine in our hearts to give us the light of the knowledge of the glory of God in the face of Christ."

Thanks be to God for his inexpressible gift.

Elvis after a Difficult School Year

I GREW UP DANCING to Elvis Presley, even though Mom thought he was too risqué! Dancing to Elvis was great exercise and so much fun. I still sing his songs. I once made a road trip to Memphis to visit his home. I found a hotel on Elvis Presley Parkway with 24-hour Elvis movies in the rooms, and a large guitar painted on the bottom of the swimming pool. I was in Elvis heaven for two days. I visited Graceland and wrote my name on the wall surrounding the home. I was in my mid-fifties.

We had a difficult school year in the early 2000s. When the faculty and staff met for our final in-service meeting for the year, I couldn't resist writing the opening prayer using some of Elvis's best-known songs:

When we experience **HEARTBREAK HOTEL**, please, **LOVE ME TENDER**, look for the **BLUE MOON**, and **WALK HAND IN HAND**.

WHEN YOU, GOD, GIVE US A MOUNTAIN TOO HIGH TO CLIMB, and we are feeling the pelting of the **OLD KENTUCKY RAIN**.

— 34 —

When we are hurt and when we are **ALL SHOOK UP, DON'T BE CRUEL,** and please **DON'T STEP ON MY BLUE SUEDE SHOES.**

When we are **HOUND DOGS,** let us try to see one another as **TEDDY BEARS.**

And when we are **DOWN AT THE END OF LONELY STREET, TREAT ME NICE.**

WE CAN'T GO ON WITH SUSPICIOUS MINDS, so let there be **PEACE IN THE VALLEY.**

When the **BLACK STAR IS OVER OUR SHOULDER,** let us shine on one another, and let us always remember that **EVERY STAR IS TO MAKE WISHES,** and we **HAVE TO PATCH IT UP,** all the differences among us. Our time to work together is **NOW OR NEVER.**

Help us, Lord our God, say in the midst of it all, **GLORY, GLORY HALLE-LUIA, O GOD, HOW GREAT THOU ART.**

Transformation

WHEN I LIVED in New Orleans I often wandered an hour away up the Mississippi coast to the small towns of Long Beach and Pass Christian to walk the beach, away from the lack of anonymity in New Orleans, "where everyone knows your name." I always looked for my favorite live oak tree bending over the street by the water.

Shortly after Katrina and Rita swept through the coast, I drove up to the shore and found almost total destruction – homes and businesses gone, oak trees uprooted and the beach deserted and even the sea gulls were gone. I went in search of my favorite oak tree. I was looking for one thing but I found something else. The tree was gone but out of its remaining trunk, an artist with the eyes of hope, had created the most exquisite beach sculptures – of sea turtles, pelicans, herons and dolphins. I was awed by the beauty of it and that one person with the eyes of hope could take something so dead, so drowned, and create a symbol of hope and transformation for all who pass by.

My hope is that each of us will see with the eyes of an artist and create new life wherever there has been destruction and become lights shining in dark places.

Gifts My Father Gave Me

WHEN I WAS IN PUBLIC SCHOOL in middle and high school, I was in the marching band. I played the clarinet and snare drum. Many years later when I was a young RSCJ teaching at Woodlands Academy in Lake Forest, Illinois, my father called and said he was in the area and he had a gift for me. He pulled up into the circle drive and unloaded a set of six drums that a client had given him because the client couldn't pay the bill for the fertilizer Dad had sold to him. We couldn't afford a set of drums when I was in the marching band, but Dad always promised me that someday I would have a set of drums. Dad was always faithful to his promises. He was like the 'other wise man'. Dad's journey took longer than many, but he always took care of us.

When I was with Dad in the Gardner, Kansas, cemetery, visiting our deceased family members, I noticed an empty plot, and I asked him who it was for. "That one is for you," he replied. I had no idea that he had purchased a burial spot for me, just in case there was no room for me in the Society of the Sacred Heart cemeteries. A year before Dad died in November 1989, he bought me a second hand set of left-handed golf clubs because I could never learn to play golf right-handed. After he died I discovered that he had maintained a life insurance policy for me (just in case I left our congregation), even when he could not afford to maintain his own health insurance premiums.

When Mom died at Christmas time, our family once again gathered at the Gardner cemetery. After saying our final farewell to Mom, everyone returned to their homes, and Dad and I drove back to his home in Storm Lake, Iowa. We gathered in the

tree lit living room, and he reached down and gave me the gifts he had wrapped for Mom. One was a digital watch. I wore it for years but I could never learn to set the time when I moved from one time zone to another. Dad could make anything work. That is one gift my father did not give me.

I will always be grateful for the gifts my father gave me: my life, a set of drums, a burial plot, a life insurance policy, a set of golf clubs, a digital watch. But most of all, I always remember his great laugh, his love of solitude, his father's love, and his faith that a star was guiding him even when his dreams did not work out the way he hoped. When I listen to marching bands, my heart leaps, and I say, "Thank you, Dad, for all your gifts and for teaching me how to march to my own drum."

He gave me one final gift. When he was dying in 1989, we asked him for one final favor. Mom died at Christmas time; our brother Chuck died during Holy Week. We asked him not to die on Thanksgiving, the only holiday free from sadness and loss. Thanksgiving came and went. He died two days later on my fiftieth birthday. Dad always kept his promises.

What lasting gifts do you give your children? What gifts will they remember? Ask them.

The Miller Family

MOM AND DAD were great parents. They raised their four children: Mary Dell, Chuck, Shirley and Carolyn in small towns in Nebraska and Iowa. Because of Dad's business, we moved several times. Mom worked full time. We all had our chores.

Mine was the family ironing. We were a happy family, growing up in a household of love and faith and goodness and generosity. We learned the meaning of hard work and sharing of responsibilities and the importance of laughter and family prayer together.

The Miller home was the place our friends gathered: dancing in the living room after school to American Bandstand or playing Kick the Can in the evening and eating Mom's delicious popcorn. We lived right off a highway, and "hobos" rode the trains and often stopped in Tekamah, Nebraska, where we lived with their knapsacks on their backs. Mom befriended them and often left meals on our front porch for them. Meeting them was my first real experience of homelessness and feeding the hungry. Mom was a great teacher.

The three sisters are so different in many ways: Mary Dell, wife, mother, grandmother, educator, volunteer, and a clothing designer with her own label; Carolyn, an Army wife, mother, grandmother, educator and volunteer; and Shirley, a Religious of the Sacred Heart. We are all grateful graduates of Duchesne College of the Sacred Heart in Omaha, and we cherish our Sacred Heart tradition and the faith we so easily share with one another. We share a beautiful history and a great love and respect for one another.

Mom died in 1978. Chuck died in 1981. Dad died in 1989. Mary Dell lived in California; Carolyn outside Omaha, and I was living in New Orleans. The three sisters decided that we couldn't just meet at our family funerals, and that we needed to see one another at least once a year. Thus, began our annual reunions as sisters and best friends.

We have all of Mom's handwritten, food stained recipe cards, and while we are together we bake her cookies and fudge and prepare her special meals. Mary Dell and Carolyn are the cooks and bakers. I am the griller. I was always too busy ironing to learn culinary skills from Mom! It is always a beautiful time for us – sharing our lives, praying together, remembering, being grateful, swimming, taking walks, watching good movies, drinking good California wine, and seeing nieces and nephews.

Of all the gifts God has given me, family is first on my list.

Baptist Seminarians

I WENT OUT to Lake Pontchartrain for a morning of prayer and reflection. I was sitting on a bench facing the Lake with my Bible and journal in my lap. I looked up and two young men sat down beside me and asked me what I was doing. I told them. They said they had been watching me. They were two Baptist seminarians, with a day off, and pockets filled with Scripture quotes. They wanted to know the real truth about the CATHOLIC FAITH. For the next hour we talked about prayer, forgiveness, salvation, redemption, conversion, sacraments. It was a delightful conversation. When they departed they gave me a little Baptist book of Scripture quotes. As they left I opened the little book and the first quotation was from St. Paul, "Be hospitable to strangers, for you may be entertaining angels unaware."

What did these two enthusiastic young men teach me: to be open to the unexpected, to see interruptions as grace, to share our stories, to learn from one another and yes, to always be hospitable for angels are all around us.

Corn Cob in Newly Fallen Snow

SEVERAL YEARS AGO I was making my annual retreat at Sacred Heart Jesuit Retreat House in Sedalia, Colorado in the foothills of the Rockies. I was in a discernment process about next steps in my life. I knew I needed to make a change but it was unclear what ministry would be next for me.

A heavy snow had fallen. I put on my boots and jacket and gloves and went out for a walk in the newly fallen snow. I walked a few steps and looked down and in front of me was an empty corn cob lying in the snow, illuminated with light. All the corn had been eaten by the squirrels, but they left the cob for me. "Ah! That is how I feel!" In a Midwestern metaphor, "There is no more corn on this cob."

That moment helped me find the words for what I was experiencing and filled me with peace and the freedom to listen deeply to what God would be saying to me during the days to come.

The corn cob became the theme of my retreat and led me to a momentous change in my life – one for which I will always be grateful.

I love corn on the cob, and I can never eat it without thanking the squirrels for the gift they left behind for me.

Kissing Deer

LATE AFTERNOON IN NOVEMBER is one of my favorite times of the year, especially in the foothills of the Rocky Mountains. I was making my retreat at Sacred Heart Jesuit Retreat House in Sedalia, Colorado. I was sitting by the little stream running through the property flowing from the statue of the Sacred Heart, "From His Heart shall flow streams of living water." A golden glow covered the mountains and trees. I heard a rustle in the trees behind me. I turned and a deer came out of the bushes, looked cautiously at me and went to the stream to drink. I sat very still. Soon another deer came out of the bushes on the other side of the stream and came to drink. And then the most beautiful thing happened. They crossed the stream toward one another and kissed. I couldn't move. I felt I was witnessing a wonder and that God was giving me a glimpse of how the world was meant to be, how God created it to be, to cross streams, to reach across to one another, to bridge our differences, to share our streams, our tenderness, our compassion, our kindness, to greet one another with a holy kiss.

> Love and kindness now meet,
> justice and peace shall kiss,
> kindness reaches up from the earth
> and justice leans down from heaven.
> —*Psalm 85*

Those two deer, an unexpected gift from the trees, beside the stream, have been a symbol of compassion to me, reminding me that I, too, am invited daily to spread this kind of gentleness and kindness each and every day, many times a day. I had my camera with me and captured that moment on film as well as in my heart lest I forget what they taught me that day by the stream in late November.

As John Muir, naturalist wrote many years ago, "No wonder the hills and groves were God's first temple."

Easter Candle

A FORMER STUDENT wrote recently and sent me a quote she thought I could use for an article or prayer service, "When you blow out my candle, it doesn't make yours burn any brighter." It is Easter, and our churches are filled with candle light. The Easter candle burns brightly. "Accept this Easter candle, a flame divided but undimmed, a pillar of fire that glows to the honor of God. Let it mingle with the lights of heaven and continue bravely burning to dispel the darkness. May the morning star which never sets find this flame still burning…"

Have I allowed the light of Christ to enter into and transform darkness in my life?

Have I blown out the light from anyone's candle, hoping mine would burn more brightly?

Have I been light for others, by my words, my love, my support, my encouragement?

Do I dispel darkness or do I create it?

There are people all around us whose candle is burning dimly because of sickness, illness, pain, loss, failure, displacement. How can I help their candle to burn more brightly?

Let us pray that we will be light for one another, that we will never dim the light of another's candle or in the words of Isaiah, "A bruised reed he will not break; a dimly burning wick, she will not quench." Let us ask ourselves, "Will my candle grow any brighter because I have snuffed yours out or will there be more light in the world when our flames grow side by side?"

Section 3

Society of the Sacred Heart

Saint Madeleine Sophie Barat's Vision

WHO WAS THIS WOMAN? Madeleine Sophie Barat? Why does she remain so important for us today 220 years after she began the Society of the Sacred Heart? She has provided us with a spirituality of transformation that is as important today, if not more so, than it was in 1800.

Her driving force in her long life was God's love lavishly poured out on the world, and her direct experience of that love in her life, and her desire that everyone would know and experience the personal, intimate love of God, of the Heart of Christ, a love so profound that it would transform peoples and societies. Her gift to the Church, her charism, was a way of life and a spiritual path of glorifying the Heart of Jesus, discovering and revealing God's love. The charism can be summed up in a single word, in the words of Jesus: LOVE. It is all about love; it was in the beginning, is now and ever shall be. She experienced the love streaming from the Heart of Christ, through our own hearts and out to the children of families and out into the world – the single most important influence in transforming the world of 1800 and 2020.

Madeleine Sophie Barat began something so inspired that it has reached to the four corners of the world, "Go therefore, and make disciples of every nation, and know that I am with you until the end of time" (Gospel of Matthew 28). The spirituality we have received from her is an incarnational spirituality, to see God in all creation, the God of love, the open Heart of Christ, the pierced Heart of God, embracing the pierced heart of humanity.

The Book of Wisdom speaks of God "trodding the earth, yet touching the heavens." That has always been a powerful image for me – God in our midst, both imminent and transcendent, in the mess and the magic, in the valley of tears and the peaks of joy, in the vineyards and in the noise of the city, contemplative in touching the heavens, active in transforming the earth.

I read once that "the Heart of Jesus is the only place big enough for the whole world." The Heart of Jesus is where Madeleine Sophie Barat drew her inspiration and lived her life, for the sake of the world and where we, the family of the Sacred Heart, continue to draw our inspiration today. She often said, "Let love be your life for all eternity." Let us all continue to live her vision.

St. Madeleine Sophie Barat and St. Rose Philippine Duchesne

Saints in the Society of the Sacred Heart

WHO WERE THESE two women?

Philippine was from a large and wealthy, political family, living in a city apartment in Grenoble, France. Sophie was from a simpler family, her father a barrel maker. Sophie played in the vineyards behind her home in Joigny, France. Philippine played in the courtyard of the Palace of Justice, looking up at the majestic French Alps. Sophie was home-schooled by her brother Louis Barat. Philippine was a boarder at St. Marie d'en Haut, the Visitandine monastery in Grenoble.

Sophie who in her younger years wanted to be a contemplative Carmelite. Philippine longed to be a missionary.

They both lived by rivers - Philippine by the rushing River Isere running through Grenoble. Sophie by the River Yonne meandering through Joigny.

The two of them provide us with the wholeness of the vision of the Society of the Sacred Heart:

We need both the simplicity of the vineyards and the grandeur of the Alps.

We need politics and barrel making, mountain climbing and vine growing.

We need both kinds of rivers — meandering and rushing.

We need the stability, confidence and contemplative spirit of Sophie, and the courage and missionary spirit of Philippine.

Sophie was called Child of Fire; Philippine known as the Heart of Oak. An unbeatable team — fire and oak — setting the world ablaze with the love of the Heart of Jesus.

There is a living water that runs through the Society of the Sacred Heart — the living water flowing from the Heart of Christ. It is the love of the Heart of Jesus, the great Society tradition 220 years old, formed out of a vision of a young woman, Madeleine Sophie Barat, in a wounded world with the Heart of Jesus as its healer; it is a love that bridges continents, nationalities, races, centuries. It is the living water flowing through our lives, through the undertow and the swift currents, the ebb and the flow, the times of drought and the times of plenty.

I personally believe that living by the rivers deeply influenced Sophie and Philippine and their understanding of devotion to Sacred Heart of Jesus. Whenever I sit by the river, whether it is the great Mississippi or the muddy Missouri, I am grateful to them for leading me to a deeper understanding of the love flowing from Heart of Jesus.

Prayer for Sacred Heart Graduates

WE PRAY FOR YOU as you leave Sacred Heart:

- That the fire of God's love, as expressed in the Heart of Christ, will permeate everything you do and all that you are
- That you will be men and women of prayer, with a deep faith in God, in yourselves, in others, in our world, which is entrusted to your care
- That your minds and hearts will be filled with dreams, dreams that you can return to over and over again when the struggles of life drag you down
- That you will not only think things through, but that you will pray them through, listening to the voice of the Holy Spirit
- That you will be lifelong learners, whose hearts and minds and souls are constantly thirsting to know more, be more, love more and believe more
- That you will continually discover your own unique God-given gifts and have the courage to share them because the world will have an empty space until you do
- That you will be women and men who risk, who because you are people of prayer and of service, because you take time to wonder, that you will hear the inner voices, voices that challenge you to right the wrong, to lead with light, to care with compassion, to be witnesses to the Resurrection
- I pray that you will be flexible and adaptable, who, like the windswept cypress at the ocean's edge, can bend but not break

- That you will continue your commitment to community outreach, reaching out and learning from those who have less than we do, and yet in some ways more than we do, and that you will learn from them
- That you will be witnesses to wonder and will take time out of your busy lives to sit by a quiet mountain stream, to photograph a sunset, to write a poem, to wish upon a star, to walk gently upon the earth, and that you be grateful recipients of the quiet whispers of God's daily gifts
- That you will be incarnational women and men who find God in every moment and who see the person next to you as THE WORD MADE FLESH
- That you will reverence each person you meet and walk gently on the earth
- That you will leave here knowing that Sacred Heart is not just a school but a way of life, a gift to be lived and shared for the rest of your life
- Most of all, I pray that you will be witnesses to the love of Heart of Jesus, the end, mission and purpose of Sacred Heart education. "Let love be your life for all eternity" [—St. Madeleine Sophie Barat].

Acknowledgments

- I wish to thank my sisters, Mary Dell and Carolyn, who suggested this book and encouraged me all of my life.
- All the people I have met along the way who have inspired me.
- The Society of the Sacred Heart, the family of the Sacred Heart, and all those I have worked with who have taught me to pay attention.
- Frances Gimber, RSCJ, for editing, and book designer, Peggy Nehmen, for her creative talent.

CPSIA information can be obtained
at www.ICGtesting.com
Printed in the USA
LVHW011051251120
672429LV00001B/1